Green Business Basics

"We have been 'smoking' (emitting greenhouse gases) for the past 250 years, and now we have 'lung cancer' (global warming)."
—Robert Strom, *Hot House: Global Climate Change and the Human Condition*

"The consequences of climate change will depend on how the physical impacts interact with socioeconomic factors. Population movement and growth will often exacerbate the impacts by increasing society's exposure to environmental stresses and reducing the amount of resource available per person. . . ."

—*The Stern Review*

"The overwhelming message of . . . [the] *Stern Review* on the economics of climate change is that it is now time to move on from arguing about statistics to taking drastic action at an international level. . . . Even if Stern is only half right . . . the consequence of doing nothing is still so dreadful that it ought not to be contemplated."

—*The Guardian* (U.K.)

"There are no passengers on spaceship Earth. We are all crew."
—Marshall McLuhan

"We must make the rescue of the environment the central organizing principle of our civilization . . . the environment is much more than a policy position to me; it is a profoundly moral obligation. We have only one Earth. And if we do not keep it healthy and safe, every other gift we leave our children will be meaningless."

—Al Gore, 2007 Nobel Peace Prize recipient

Green Business Basics

✔ *24 Lessons for Meeting the Challenges of Global Warming*

NICK DALLAS

New York Chicago San Francisco Lisbon
London Madrid Mexico City Milan New Delhi
San Juan Seoul Singapore Sydney Toronto

1 2 3 4 5 6 7 8 9 0 DOC/DOC 0 9 8

ISBN-13: 978-0-07-160357-7
ISBN-10: 0-07-160357-3

Contents

Green Business Basics

☑ Climate change basics

Humanity's report card for the duration of the second half of the twentieth century would probably be assigned a qualified pass with significant scope for improvement, especially on the equity side. Although overshadowed by the threat of nuclear holocaust by dueling superpowers, there were no "Great Wars," but regional and local military conflicts were numerous, often quite protracted, but contained within certain geographical spheres. Significant technological, medical, and scientific breakthroughs laid the groundwork for economic advances resulting in substantial improvements in the material well-being and life expectancy of hundreds of millions. However, an even greater number in developing countries remained in an almost destitute state, divorced from this tide of rising prosperity.

This qualified progress is under threat of being derailed during the first half of the twenty-first century. The emerging risk of climate change and its associated consequences could be humanity's undoing. If climate change, triggered by higher carbon dioxide levels, does take hold this century, and we experience some of the more unpalatable and extreme scenarios, the results will be nothing short of catastrophic in human terms. Climate change will put pressure on the availability of land and allocation of resources, and it will destroy ecosystems. Food shortages, accelerated species loss, reduced availability of fresh water, and disrupted access to energy supplies will become more frequent as the planet's carrying capacity comes under stress. Quite possibly, more lives and livelihoods will be lost as a result of human conflict and disruption arising from these competitive pressures of scarcity and reduced access rather than due to the climatic impacts themselves.

This short primer aims to give the reader a basic understanding of the fundamental aspects of climate change, with the hope that these fundamentals may act as a springboard to pursuing the debate to the next level. It is imperative that we all, as global citizens, become sensitized to the debate, follow deliberations, and remain informed. Our knowledge and awareness of climate change issues will not only shape our actions, but also determine our responses to government policies enacted to deal with humanity's greatest challenge this century.

Climate change or global warming—what is the difference?

Since the weather is forever changing and this fluctuation is seen as natural, when does climate variability constitute what is termed as the problem of "climate change"? *Climate change* is defined as any substantial change in measures of climate (temperature, precipitation, wind, or other variables) lasting for an extended period (a decade or longer), whether due to natural factors or processes, or as a result of human activities.[1] In some instances, the term "climate change" is used to refer specifically to change in climate caused by human activities.

The term "global warming" is used to describe the average increase in global temperature of the atmosphere near the Earth's surface, which can occur from natural and human-induced causes.[2] Therefore, *global warming* is specific to an increase in temperature, while climate change is more encompassing and indicates that additional changes are occurring other than the increase in temperature.

Although different, the two terms are often used interchangeably because they are interlinked. Global warming is the driving force behind climate change. However, climate change is an issue because of global warming. The scientific consensus is that both lead to the same dire consequences.

✓ What is global warming?

Life exists on our planet as a result of a natural greenhouse phenomenon occurring in our atmosphere. A protective atmospheric blanket regulates the Earth's temperature, making life sustainable. Although many gases are in the Earth's atmosphere, it overwhelmingly consists of nitrogen and oxygen. However, the less-abundant, so-called "greenhouse gases" are critical in maintaining this temperature balance. Despite comprising less than 1 percent of the Earth's atmosphere, the naturally occurring greenhouse gases of mainly carbon dioxide, water vapor, ozone, methane, and nitrous oxide are largely responsible for keeping the Earth warm. As the Earth's surface warms, it emits long-wave infrared radiation back into space. Not all this radiation reaches space, as its passage is impeded by atmospheric greenhouse gases that trap and re-emit it, leading to the warming of the lower atmosphere.

Of the greenhouse gases, carbon dioxide, comprising 0.03–0.04 percent of the atmosphere, and water vapor are the two most important. The estimate is that the absence of these two gases would suppress the current natural greenhouse mechanism in place and would plunge the Earth's average temperature to around –20°C. The phenomenon of global warming is attributed to substantial increases in the Earth's atmosphere of greenhouse gases—in particular carbon dioxide—resulting from the burning of fossil fuels and deforestation, both human-induced activities. The higher greenhouse gas concentrations are believed to lead to higher average global temperatures and rising sea levels. A report published by the Intergovernmental Panel on Climate Change (IPCC) states that clear evidence exists that during the twentieth century, sea levels have risen by 20 cm and average global temperatures by 0.6°C. The IPCC further predicts that if atmospheric greenhouse gas levels continue to rise as a result of unmodified human activities, rising temperatures and sea levels will also be accompanied by less-predictable weather patterns. Extreme climatic events, such as floods, droughts, and storms, are expected to occur with greater intensity.

"All across the world, in every kind of environment and region known to man, increasingly dangerous weather patterns and devastating storms are abruptly putting an end to the long-running debate over whether or not climate change is real. Not only is it real, it's here, and its effects are giving rise to a frighteningly new global phenomenon: the man-made natural disaster."

—Barack Obama, Democrat Senator

"We are living on this planet as if we had another one to go to."

—Terri Swearingen, 1997 Goldman Environmental Prize recipient

☐ There are other
atmospheric gases

☑ The importance of greenhouse gases

Although water vapor is considered the most important greenhouse gas in the regulation of the greenhouse effect, its atmospheric concentration is not changing directly as a result of human activities. For this reason, water vapor does not occupy the same high-profile role that other greenhouse gases do in the climate change debate. The focus has been principally on such greenhouse gases as carbon dioxide, methane, nitrous oxide, ozone, and chlorofluorocarbons (CFCs), whose concentrations have been increasing as a result of human activities and providing the impetus for an enhanced greenhouse effect.

The importance of greenhouse gases lies in their radiative absorbing and emitting properties that provide a protective blanketing effect in our atmosphere. When discussing greenhouse gases, climate scientists often use the terms "radiative forcing" and "global warming potential" or GWP. *Radiative forcing* is a measure used to describe to what extent a gas alters the balance of incoming and outgoing energy in the atmosphere. If positive, as in the case of greenhouse gases, it implies that the gas has a warming effect on the atmosphere. *GWP* is simply a multiple reflecting the radiative forcing properties of any gas, where carbon dioxide is considered the benchmark and assigned a value of one. The common greenhouse gases all have GWPs greater than that of CO_2. However, CO_2 is what has the greatest radiative-forcing effect (warming ability) and it continues to occupy an ever-expanding role in the climate change debate. A single molecule of CO_2 does not have the same capability to warm the atmosphere as other greenhouse gas molecules. Its radiative-forcing potency is derived from its abundance and longevity (an atmospheric lifetime between 50 and 200 years).

After carbon dioxide, methane is the next major contributor to global warming. Although the atmospheric lifetime of methane is only 12 years, its global warming potential is more than 20 times that of carbon dioxide. Methane is emitted naturally by many sources, but it's also emitted by human activities: natural gas use, landfills, rice, and livestock farming. Enormous quantities of methane are locked up in deep-seafloor oceanic sediments and permafrost. Fears exist that the warming of oceans (they are carbon sinks[3]) and melting of permafrost have the potential to unlock these enormous methane deposits, exacerbating climate change.

"Our planet would be largely uninhabitable if it wasn't for the heat-regulating role of greenhouse gases."

The Perfect Couple.

☐ Why not methane?

☑ Focusing on carbon dioxide

Why has the climate change debate centered on the role of carbon dioxide? The study of past climate has revealed a closely linked relationship between atmospheric carbon-dioxide levels and global climate. The greater the amount of heat-trapping greenhouse gases in the atmosphere, the higher the temperature. Scientists have drilled down more than three kilometers, and they have taken ice cores from Greenland and Antarctic ice sheets. Air bubbles are trapped inside this "ancient ice." By determining the greenhouse gas composition of these air bubbles, one can develop a snapshot of past atmospheres. Further examination of oxygen and hydrogen isotopes in these ice cores yields estimates of the temperature at which this ice formed. These studies show a frightening correlation between temperature and greenhouse gas levels.

The focus has been on carbon dioxide, one of the more abundant greenhouse gases, because of its atmospheric longevity, and because its atmospheric levels have been increasing alarmingly since the Industrial Revolution of the eighteenth century. From preindustrial levels of 280 ppm (parts per million), present levels are at more than 370 ppm. The estimate is that 70 percent of the enhanced greenhouse effect can be attributed to this increase of CO_2.[4] This represents an increase of more than 30 percent or 160 billion tons of CO_2, which can mainly be attributed to the burning of fossil fuels. Anthropogenic (human-derived) influences have been the main contributors to increasing atmospheric carbon dioxide levels during the last few hundred years.

The ever-increasing prodigious quantities of carbon dioxide spurted into the atmosphere, combined with its lengthy atmospheric lifetime, have hastened global warming. Climatic conditions on the planet Venus in some ways can be considered an outcome of a runaway greenhouse effect. Venus has a surface temperature of over 400°C and its atmosphere comprises 96 percent carbon dioxide by volume. The Earth's advantage is that it has carbon sinks (oceans, soils, vegetation, and so forth), which absorb carbon dioxide. These carbon sinks do not have limitless capacities and may reach saturation levels. All this highlights the urgency of curbing carbon dioxide emissions.

"Two of carbon dioxide's life-sustaining functions are its roles in photosynthesis and regulating the greenhouse effect. Global warming, driven by increasing carbon dioxide levels, will distort these two functions long-term. It is an example of having too much of a good thing."

☐ Climate change is independent of human activity

☑ Link between human activity and climate change

Being a multidisciplinary subject, surrounded by controversy and linked to a myriad of sensitive matters, climate change has attracted its fair share of skeptics in political, business, and scientific communities. The controversy is not over rising carbon dioxide levels. Since industrialization, carbon dioxide levels have been gradually increasing and this can easily be measured. The issue is whether global warming is anthropogenic in its origin.

Global climatic changes occur as a result of internal and external forcing mechanisms. Changes in atmospheric carbon dioxide levels due to human activities, which impact on the greenhouse effect, are an example of an *internal forcing mechanism*, whereas sunspot activity and changes to the Earth's orbit around the Sun are examples of *external forcing mechanisms*. Where doubts emerge is easy to see. It is quite a difficult task to accurately and separately account for climate change contributions because of both internal and external forcing mechanisms. Furthermore, if global warming does lead to climatic changes, do the external forcing mechanisms or does nature itself have a way of neutralizing this contribution? How does one disentangle global warming from natural climate variability? Making the link between human activity and climate change is an extremely complex matter as climate change encompasses many things with different response times. Scientists may never be able to quantify every single force that influences climate. However, they are striving to improve their models and factor in as many variables as possible. Many aspects of climate change interactions and dynamics still are not well understood and require further research (for example, the influence of clouds).

Much of the scientific work on climate change is carried out through computer simulation of the physics of climate. Very sophisticated models have been developed, and continue to be improved, that simulate conditions over long periods of time.

Calibration of the models takes place by running past climate conditions and comparing these model results with what happened in those past years. After calibration, climatic conditions for the next 20, 50, or 100 years can be simulated.

By studying ice cores, glacial movements, tree ring patterns, vegetation, and sea level fluctuations, various inferences can be made about climatic changes over time. Most of the evidence associating human activities with climate change is, therefore, indirect and inferred from changes in indicators that reflect climate. Despite knowledge gaps in certain areas, by focusing research on reconstructing past climates, the scientific community has developed an overwhelming consensus that global warming is already happening and is driven by human activities.[5]

"We are upsetting the atmosphere upon which all life depends. In the late '80s, when I began to take climate change seriously, we referred to global warming as a 'slow-motion catastrophe'—one we expected to kick in perhaps generations later. Instead, the signs of change have accelerated alarmingly . . . we are playing Russian roulette with features of the planet's atmosphere that will profoundly impact generations to come. How long are we willing to gamble?"

—David Suzuki, Canadian environmentalist

☐ The relationship is well known

☑The relationship is not fully understood

The most worrying thing about climate change is that scientists cannot be sure of the exact response of the world's climate system to global warming. They can only speculate and attempt to model scenarios. Assuming increasing carbon dioxide levels is the principal forcing mechanism: In what way will average global temperatures rise? Is the relationship linear, where a gradual increase in one factor will lead to a gradual increase in the other? Alternatively, the response might be muted if a natural buffer system is in operation, where rising carbon dioxide levels have only a limited impact on global temperatures. This is an argument pushed by many skeptics: nature's adaptability, where it constantly adjusts and establishes new equilibrium positions. Nature may well settle into a new equilibrium position, but the question is whether humans and other living species will tolerate this new level. Furthermore, the initial climatic response may well be muted, but this could only be a delay stage, after which a nonlinear response kicks in where temperatures rise rapidly.

Another scenario is the threshold response. Initially, there is very little response to carbon dioxide forcing until a critical threshold or tipping point is reached. The temperature then increases abruptly, stabilizing at a much higher threshold. This is quite a dangerous scenario. A 5°C increase could have a devastating effect on our planet. Studies of past climates have shown that a shift of over 5°C can occur within several decades, which is a rather miniscule period in the context of geological time. Such a cataclysmic scenario is difficult to model. It could even affect the nature of oceanic currents, thus totally distorting global weather patterns. The Hollywood film, *The Day After Tomorrow*, gave a dramatized perspective of this scenario.

It may be prudent to prepare for more damaging scenarios. Some recent studies have indicated that the Earth's climate may be more responsive to greenhouse gases than previously thought, because of the existence of amplifying feedback mechanisms. This means that impacts predicted to occur later on in this century will occur sooner. With the outlook being so uncertain, early action and intervention is the most suitable response.

"The paleoclimate record shouts out to us that, far from being self-stabilizing, the Earth's climate system is an ornery beast, which overreacts to even small nudges."
—Wallace Broecker, climate scientist, 1995

"We live on a planet whose climate is dominated by positive feedbacks, which are capable of taking us to dramatically different conditions. . . . We are on the precipice of climate system tipping points beyond which there is no redemption."
—James Hansen, Director of Goddard Institute for Space Studies (NASA)

☑ IPCC

In 1988 two United Nations organizations, the World Meteorological Organization (WMO) and the United Nations Environment Program (UNEP), established the Intergovernmental Panel on Climate Change (IPCC) to evaluate the risk of climate change brought about by human activities. It is regarded as the UN's authoritative panel on climate change matters. The IPCC itself neither carries out any research nor does it monitor any climate and related phenomena. The main activity of the IPCC is to publish special reports on topics relevant to the implementation of the UN Framework Convention on Climate Change (UNFCCC). The Kyoto Protocol has arisen out of the UNFCCC's implementation.

Peer-reviewed and published scientific literature forms the basis of IPCC's assessment reports. Its stated aims[6] are to assess scientific information relevant to:

1. human-induced climate change
2. impacts of human-induced climate change
3. options for adaptation and mitigation

The IPCC is organized into three working groups that have areas of responsibility reflecting the three previous aims. It also has a large task force responsible for calculating the volume of greenhouse gases produced by each country. IPCC's summary reports for policymakers draw considerable media attention. Some conclusions of a recent Fourth Assessment Report, published in early 2007, are that:

(i) the warming of the climate system is unequivocal
(ii) the probability that this warming is caused by natural climatic processes alone is less than 5 percent.

More than 400 experts from over 120 countries are involved in drafting, revising, and finalizing these reports, while another 2,500 experts participate in the review process. In October 2007, the IPCC was jointly awarded the Nobel Peace Prize with Al Gore for their efforts in promoting climate change awareness.

"Despite the impediments of its clumsy and cumbersome structure, its repeated rounds of report-drafting, its overextended consultation with governments and experts, the IPCC has managed to issue unequivocal statements on the dangers of climate change and the need to act urgently."

—Wikipedia

☐ ~~Kyoto has failed~~

☑ Kyoto Protocol, an important first step

Containing global warming is an endeavor that demands significant cuts in greenhouse gas emissions. Delivering these cuts is contentious because of their economic implications. The Kyoto Protocol in 1997 emerged as a global effort to achieve these reductions and limit the impact of global warming by having industrialized nations commit to emission reductions of 5.2 percent on their 1990 levels by 2008–12. It arose out of the UNFCCC, which itself was created at the Rio Earth Summit in 1992. In July 2001, 186 countries signed and ratified the Kyoto Protocol. Although it participated in climate negotiations, the United States was one of the few countries not to ratify this legal treaty. This may be considered a flaw in the treaty, as the United States is among the world's largest polluters. Many inside the United States feel discomfort at Washington's stance. Several states, such as California, are setting their own emission standards and American businesses are seeking emission targets and tradeable permits to factor in future risk.

In achieving reduction targets, six greenhouse gases are targeted and the Protocol sanctions three flexible mechanisms: international emissions trading (discussed on pages 37–39), joint implementation, and the Clean Development Mechanism (CDM). The joint implementation mechanism allows *Annex 1 countries* (that is, developed and transition economies) to earn emission reduction units by participating in joint projects with other Annex 1 countries.

In the CDM, Annex 1 countries receive emission reduction credits by financing projects in *non-Annex 1 countries* (developing countries that are not obliged to carry out emission cuts). These cuts have been negotiated under a framework of "common but differentiated responsibilities," which acknowledge that the largest share of historical and current greenhouse gas emissions has originated in developed countries and the global share of emissions originating in developing countries must have some capacity to grow to meet their social and development needs. The CDM has also attracted some criticism. One viewpoint is it legitimizes the polluting legacy of developed Annex 1 countries by allowing them to buy their way out of emission reductions. A fairer assessment should probably consider the overall quality of the project, where the socioeconomic impact on the beneficiary community is examined as well as the level and nature of emission reductions.

Kyoto remains the bedrock of any credible strategy going forward. It expires in 2012. Only time will reveal the exact nature of the new global framework post-Kyoto. Goals would be to have emissions trading entrenched and to have all significant emitter countries (both developed and developing) ratify any new agreement.

"The Clean Development Mechanism provides an important channel of private sector participation in financing low-carbon investments in developing countries."
—The Stern Review

"The Kyoto Protocol is only the first, rather modest, step. Much, much deeper emission reductions will be needed in future. The political implications are mind-blowing."
—Michael Meacher, UK Environment Minister, November 2000

☑ *The Stern Review*

The Stern Review on the Economics of Climate Change is a 700-page report released on October 30, 2006, by prominent economist Sir Nicholas Stern at the behest of the British government. Stern, the Head of the UK Government Economic Service and a former Chief Economist of the World Bank, was asked to lead a major review on the economics of climate change to acquire a better understanding of the nature of economic challenges and how they can be met globally. Although not the first economic report of its kind, this is by far the most comprehensive, accessible, and well known.

The report's main conclusion is that 1 percent of global gross domestic product (GDP) per annum is required to be invested to avoid the worst effects of climate change. This would achieve a level of stabilization at or below 550 ppm CO_2 equivalent[7] where emissions peak in the next ten years, but then need to decline between 1 and 3 percent per annum until

33

2050. Failure to make this level of investment could lead to global GDP being 20 percent lower than it might be otherwise. The report also describes climate change as potentially the greatest and widest-ranging market failure the world has seen. It offers policy prescriptions on how to go about minimizing economic and social disruptions that may arise. Although certain aspects and assumptions of the report have been criticized by some commentators and economists, the majority have commented favorably and consider its publication a watershed event.

The Stern Review's main achievement is this: it demolished the argument that action on climate change would hurt the economy. It argued that the economy would benefit in a multitude of ways and failure to act now would have considerable unintended consequences in the immediate future.

"*The Stern Review* makes clear that the question is not whether we can afford to act, but whether we can afford not to act."
—Joseph Stiglitz, Nobel Prize for Economics (2001) recipient

"The world would be foolish to neglect this strong but strictly time-bound practical message."
—Amartya Sen, Nobel Prize for Economics (1998) recipient

"Future generations may come to regard the apocalyptic report by Sir Nicholas Stern . . . as the turning point in combating global warming, or as the missed opportunity . . . he has ripped up the last excuse for inaction."

—*Independent*

"*The Stern Review* makes two invaluable contributions. The first is that it recasts environmentalism as economics. . . . Stern's second serious contribution is to provide a formula for durable environmentalism, one which binds business and government."

—*Times*

☑ Pollution represents market failure

Economics 101 teaches us that pollution is a negative externality and markets can be deficient when it comes to the provision of public goods. Society at large is disadvantaged when polluters do not pay for their pollution-generating activities. Runaway global warming and unpredictable climate change will be the ultimate price to be paid if no attempt is made to restrict carbon dioxide emissions from fossil fuel use.

One way of addressing this concern is to impose caps on emissions through a "cap and trade" system. This is done by assigning emission obligations at the national government level under the Kyoto Protocol. This national responsibility can be devolved to the industry level by governments placing emission caps on firms. A polluting firm is provided with carbon credits, which are simply permits to emit a given quantity of carbon dioxide. Once allocated a given number of permits, a firm's maximum pollution level is fixed. It can only expand by either becoming more energy efficient and not exceeding its permissible emissions or buying carbon credits from other firms, allowing it to increase its pollution level.

Carbon credits are tradable instruments with a transparent price. A firm cannot expand without incurring a carbon cost. However, a firm has the incentive to become more energy efficient either to avoid incurring this cost or to realize a financial gain by selling carbon credits in an open market. This trading method not only produces the least-cost option for a firm, but it also encourages the pursuit of innovative abatement technologies.

Many have proposed that imposing a carbon tax, rather than a cap and trade emission scheme, is a more efficient way of constraining polluters. Both approaches have pros and cons. The risk of a carbon tax is this: if it is not set at the right level, no guarantee exists that emissions will stabilize at or below a target level. There is precedence with a cap and trade scheme. This technique was successfully employed in reducing sulphur dioxide and nitrous oxide emissions in combating acid rain concerns. The experience of the EU Emissions Trading Scheme indicates that teething problems and fine-tuning are to be expected as individual nations try to implement carbon cap and trade schemes. Nevertheless, the cap and trade technique remains the method of preference for policymakers moving forward. Although one can expect a proliferation of national carbon markets in the near future as governments come under pressure to address climate change, a single global carbon market is a long way off.

"This is the greatest market failure the world has seen. . . . There is still time to avoid the worst impacts of climate change, if we take strong action now."

—Sir Nicholas Stern

☐ All countries are
equally vulnerable

☑ Developing countries are more vulnerable to climate change

As the level of greenhouse gas emissions is both consumption-dependent and lifestyle-driven, it comes as no surprise that the developed world has been and continues to be the principal emitter. The United States has generated 30 percent of all emissions to date and is producing about 20 percent of current annual totals, despite having only 5 percent of the world's population. In terms of per capita greenhouse emissions, Australia leads the way as a result of its heavy reliance on coal to generate electricity. China, with more than one-fifth of the world's inhabitants, has just overtaken the United States with respect to annual emissions. This gap will widen if its spectacular economic ascendancy continues.

The Kyoto Protocol recognizes the leading polluting role of industrialized nations and has assigned respective country emission targets to reflect this. The developing world is given some breathing space as its emissions on a per capita basis are a fraction of those of the developed world. It needs to hasten economic development out of necessity, to lift its citizens out of poverty, and to afford them access to basic goods and services, which those in industrialized nations take for granted.

The irony and injustice of climate change is that those who have been least responsible are the most susceptible to its impacts. Inhabitants in developing nations remain extremely vulnerable as a result of geography and economics. Many live in low-lying areas in danger from sea-level risings. They do not have the financial resources, and neither do their governments, to respond adequately to climate change. Many rely on agriculture. More pronounced extreme climatic events (droughts, floods) will lower resistance to pests and disease. Crop yields to a large extent are sensitive to prevailing climatic conditions (temperature, rainfall patterns). Agricultural productivity will invariably be affected.

People's adaptive capacity to climate change only extends as far as their resources and knowledge allow. In this respect, the developing world is disproportionately disadvantaged.

Developed nations have an obligation to assist their less-developed counterparts. This can be done in a variety of ways:

- Accelerating technology transfer and knowledge flows to help mitigate climate change.
- Participating in more CDM programs by bankrolling reforestation, renewable energy, and other projects.
- Improving disaster preparedness and management programs.

"Developing countries are especially vulnerable to the physical impacts of climate change because of their exposure to an already fragile environment, an economic structure that is highly sensitive to an adverse and changing climate, and low incomes that constrain their ability to adapt . . . climate change will increase worldwide deaths from malnutrition and heat stress. Vector-borne diseases such as malaria and dengue fever could become more widespread if effective control measures are not in place."
—*The Stern Review*

"Any future global climate change agreement that does not recognize the developing world's fight against poverty is doomed to failure."
—Opinion attributed to Tom Athanasiou, Director of American think tank, Ecoequity

☐ ~~Climate change is an environmental conspiracy~~

☑ Manufactured uncertainty

Fortunately, the debate on whether climate change is real or not is essentially over, although a small hardcore minority of "deniers" still exert some influence on the public debate. The public at large and the scientific community have embraced the irrefutable scientific evidence that climate change is happening. People are looking for solutions and awaiting an actionable agenda from governments.

However, this was not the case for some time. A well-financed and even better-connected group of skeptics, mimicking many of the tactics of the tobacco industry in past battles, was able to exert a disproportionate influence on the debate as a result of

45

their lobbying efforts and media-savviness. Often financed by oil and coal interests, they hired public relations firms to propagate uncertainty by deriding climate change as an unproven theory, rather than a fact. The media's desire to offer balanced reporting as part of public debate also aided their cause by giving equal weight to their arguments, whereas peer-reviewed scientific literature contains very few papers disagreeing with the consensus that climate change is occurring. Using vague arguments, such as "the level of warming is insignificant or part of natural climate variation," and portraying climate change activists as environmental extremists, they were able to stall the debate and delay action. After being a keen participant in Kyoto discussions, the US pulled out with the coming to power of a new administration that was more receptive to the interests of the skeptics and their financiers.

Another tactic by the skeptics was to focus on and exaggerate small parts of the debate where uncertainties or inconsistencies existed, even though there was broad agreement on a larger principle. Most scientists agree that climate change is happening, yet many may differ on details and interpretations of certain aspects, as is the nature of scientific rigor.

The skeptics have not triumphed with their denialist agenda and climate change has become a leading public concern. The battleground has moved on and their strategies are different. As governments are under pressure from both the public and business to introduce legislation tackling climate change, the skeptics' tactics are aimed at delaying and reducing the effectiveness of such action. Arguing that certain policies are against the national interest and will cause economic damage or that all the facts are not in, they continue to offer resistance.

"Carbon dioxide: They call it pollution. We call it life."
—TV advertisement response by the Washington-based Climate Enterprise Institute on the release of Al Gore's documentary, *An Inconvenient Truth*

"It's easy to refute all the contrarian arguments but that seems to have very little effect on how commonly they are believed. Refuted arguments seem to live on in the public imagination. To bring the public on board to a rational discussion of climate policy needs more than logical argument."
—Michael Tobis, Ph.D., University of Texas Institute of Geophysics

"Ever eager for the drama of competing dogmas, the media largely ignored mainstream scientists, whose hesitations did not make good copy."
—Kerry Emanuel, *What We Really Know About Climate Change*

☐ Let's aim for business as usual

☑ Big reductions are necessary

Presently, the overwhelming scientific consensus is that global warming is happening and it is driven by human activities. There is, however, less agreement on how much the Earth will warm and how quickly, and what atmospheric carbon dioxide levels are considered acceptable and manageable. Complicated computer models factoring a multitude of variables allow climate scientists to make forecasts and assign probabilities to scenarios, but it is impossible to quantify every variable that influences climate.

The U.K. government–initiated *Stern Review* recommends emission cuts of 60 percent by 2050 relative to 2000 levels, claiming this should keep greenhouse gas levels at or below 550 ppm CO_2 equivalent (CO_2e) and minimize any temperature

49

rise to less than 2°C. Presently, levels stand at around 430 ppm CO_2e. Others, such as journalist and environmental campaigner George Monbiot, call for much tougher cuts, recommending that developed nations cut their emissions by 90 percent by 2030. This could only be achieved by radical lifestyle changes or breakthrough technological advances.

What are the right (or acceptable) levels or targets we should aim for? No one can say with certainty. Even at our present level of 430 ppm, glaciers are retreating and extreme weather events are occurring. Biologists claim that above 500 ppm CO_2e ocean acidification occurs, putting marine ecosystems under threat. At this level, runaway heating as a result of positive feedback loops that amplify warming is possible.

With so much uncertainty, what is the true bottom line and how can we move through this maze of information? The bottom line must be that we cannot afford to get the risk analysis wrong. At stake is the planet's future and humankind's survival. This means erring on the side of caution and considering worst-case climate change scenarios as highly plausible within the next few decades. It means immediate action and an end to procrastination. It also means setting targets, deploying solutions, planning for reductions, making funds available, establishing policies, and communicating the urgency of this message. Mistakes will be made, economic resources are not infinite, and some initiatives may not turn out as effective as anticipated. An inherent risk always exists when dealing with problems of incomplete information. This approach is, however, justified, as failure to act decisively now not only exposes the planet to grave risks, but will also require devoting substantially greater resources in the future to deal with the matter.

"If you think mitigated climate change is expensive, try unmitigated climate change."
—Dr. Richard Gammon, University of Washington

"The problem is not yet insoluble, but becomes more difficult with each passing day. A goal of confining global warming to an average of 2 centigrade degrees above pre-industrial levels would be very challenging, and even this amount of warming would be likely to have some severe impacts. . . ."
—2007 Joint Science Academies' statement on growth and sustainability

"We have to choose a prudent risk level. You wouldn't fly a plane that had more than a 1 percent (one in 100) or even 0.1 percent (one in 1000) chance of crashing. We should at least be careful with the planet."

☐ ~~Reductions are cost-prohibitive~~

☑ Achieving reductions: part 1

—Avoiding Catastrophe, a survey by the Carbon Equity Project

There is no silver-bullet solution to address climate change. Many solutions are now available and widespread action will be required on multiple fronts. In broad terms, solutions to reducing atmospheric greenhouse gas levels fall into six categories: reducing consumption, modifying consumption, improving energy efficiency, optimizing the energy production mix, carbon dioxide removal/storage, and strengthening education.

Reducing consumption of goods and services by default reduces energy demand and contributes to lower carbon-dioxide emissions. It also moves profligate societies toward a more sustainable direction. Naturally, reducing consumption is very contentious in simplistic terms as it implies reduced economic activity. This is a difficult strategy to sell as our global economic system is based on increasing consumption and annually increasing economic growth. It would also be inequitable for the developing world, which is relying on increased consumption to meet its developmental goals.

Modifying consumption is more palatable for most and does not necessarily lead to reduced economic activity, only less energy-intensive activity. It could involve using public transport or cycling to work instead of driving. Substituting meat with vegetables, sourcing food locally, switching transport to LPG fuel, or using manual instead of electrically powered devices are other examples. A positive side benefit of this approach is that many activities may involve greater physical exertion and a healthier choice of foods, which may lead to health benefits.

Improving energy efficiency in manufacturing, operations, or energy production is a very attractive option for all. It is a triple-win strategy for consumers, producers, and the environment. Lowering the costs of manufacturing processes through streamlining, switching to energy-efficient light bulbs, installing insulation, more extensive recycling, improving thermal efficiencies in fossil fuel plants, and increasing conversion efficiencies in photovoltaic cells are some examples. Governments have a role to play by offering research and development incentives through grants, rebates, and favorable taxation arrangements. Achieving greater energy efficiency is a win-win strategy for business as it can simultaneously reduce operating costs and minimize carbon dioxide emissions. Energy gains can also be achieved through regulation. Legislating for new building standards that embody energy-saving design features is one approach.

"How is it that we have created an economic system that tells us it is cheaper to destroy the earth and exhaust its people than to nurture them both? Is it rational to have a pricing system which discounts the future and sells off the past? How did we create an economic system that confused capital liquidation with income?"

—Paul Hawken, *Natural Capitalism*

☑ Achieving reductions: part 2

Optimizing the energy production mix by developing low carbon and renewable energy is probably the most critical strategy in combating climate change. After all, our fossil fuel dependence is what has brought about this problem. How will we be weaned off this dependency when petroleum-fueled automobile sales show no sign of abating and coal-fired power stations dominate electricity production? How will we address the migration to the greater use of renewable and alternative fuels? In the short term, maintaining economic development will invariably require increasing energy consumption unless one's economy is significantly restructured. Achieving economic growth within environmental constraints in a sustainable emission-reducing way is a major challenge. The solutions will be diverse as countries pursue different pathways depending on their natural endowments, security concerns, and what they perceive as their domains of competitive advantage. No doubt, those with abundant coal supplies will disproportionately focus research efforts on developing clean-coal technologies. Those without fossil-fuel deposits will be pursuing alternative and renewable energy options more vigorously.

Carbon dioxide removal/storage can be achieved in a variety of ways, two being reforestation and carbon sequestration. Increasing forest and vegetation cover results in greater absorption (removal) of carbon dioxide through photosynthesis. Reforestation, although appealing, is not as simple as planting trees and is considered a temporary storage for carbon. When forests are felled, ecosystems and biodiversity are also lost. Replacing diverse ecosystems with single-species timber plantations invariably reduces biodiversity. Forests are great greenhouse gas sinks, but their management and expansion must be conscious of ecology restoration and protection. Carbon sequestration involves capturing carbon dioxide emanating from power-plant operations, and then storing it in large underground stable geological formations. The technique is still in its infancy and years away from being implemented on a large scale as there are still significant technical hurdles to overcome, including dangers of rerelease.

Strengthening education, training, and public awareness on climate change is another important strategy because it has the potential to influence human behavior. This could involve disseminating information on sustainable development that can make citizens more conscious of their actions. Conducting climate-change training and workshops for policymakers, organizing conferences, and developing web-accessible information sites are all knowledge-enhancement initiatives that augment public awareness.

"Climate change is among the most pervasive threats to the web of life, yet we have the power to address its root causes and limit its impact on the planet. Smart energy choices made by individuals and businesses can dramatically reduce CO_2 emissions and slow global warming. Without action, climate change will cause the extinction of countless species and destroy some of the world's most precious ecosystems."

—World Wildlife Fund

☐ Oil remains plentiful

☑ Challenges of transport and biofuels

Reducing transport emissions is particularly challenging. First, petroleum as a fuel source is so prominent in our daily lives and, second, transport is critical to economic activity and international trade, both drivers of prosperity. Approaches to reducing transport emissions include making transport vehicles more energy efficient by weight or size reductions and improving fuel combustion, or switching to alternative fuels. Hybrid vehicles are definitely cleaner, but their higher costs have restricted their widespread use. Plug-in electric vehicles might make inroads with advances in battery-storage technology, but what is important is that the electricity comes from decarbonized sources; otherwise, the problem is just being shift-

61

ed. Hydrogen as a fuel source at this time remains impractical, but it continues to attract research attention.

Biofuels used directly, or as part of gasoline blends, are also entering the picture. They are championed, often by politicians in rural constituencies, for their supposed capacity to reduce greenhouse gases, enhance energy security, and provide a new income stream for farmers. Except in a few instances, such as Brazil's sugarcane to ethanol program, it is highly unlikely that biofuels can create a substantial dent in petroleum consumption. Biofuels have the potential to create more problems, on top of the subsidization burden they impose on taxpayers. When more agricultural land is diverted to growing biomass feedstocks, a risk exists of higher food prices and damaging biodiversity. Generating biofuels from crops grown on marginal or degraded land, or using residual biomass materials, addresses some of the pitfalls, but it does not change the outlook that biofuels will only ever play a niche role as alternative transport fuels.

The challenge is more extensive than the nature of automobiles and fuels. The challenge is also about urban planning and design, curbing urban sprawl, improving and expanding public transport, and changing consumer habits. The urban-design decisions of today will have climate-change implications in the years ahead. It is a complex balancing act trying to achieve less car-reliant cities and encourage denser living, while maintaining housing affordability and promoting more sustainable communities.

Predicting the face of transport in a carbon-constrained world 10 or 20 years from now is difficult. Numerous solutions are available. What is lacking is the willingness and urgency to make lifestyle adjustments. Maybe seeing crude oil surpass the US $100 per barrel mark as we reach "peak oil" and production begins to decline will provide the stimulus for more people to embrace existing sustainable options.

"The rush to energy crops threatens to cause food shortages and damage biodiversity with limited benefits . . . in light of numerous concerns, the question must be asked whether the potential 'cure' offered by biofuels is worse than the disease."
—OECD Round Table on Sustainable Development, September 2007

"Sprawling urban areas are helping to make road transportation the fastest source of the carbon emissions warming the Earth's atmosphere . . . if governments do not act now, the international effort to control global warming will become much more difficult."
—Worldwatch Institute, Washington-based research organization

☐ Nuclear ~~is the answer~~

☑ Nuclear energy is problematic

In discussing nuclear energy, one is mainly referring to energy derived from *nuclear fission*, the splitting of atoms, rather than *nuclear fusion*, the coming together of atoms. Nuclear fusion is the way the sun produces its energy and, although it holds the promise of one day providing limitless energy, it is highly unlikely that we will see a nuclear fusion plant in commercial operation before the middle of this century. The technical hurdles that need to be overcome in achieving nuclear fusion are immense as they involve dealing with temperatures of millions of degrees.

The greater use of nuclear energy of the fission variety has been proposed by many as a key strategy in combating climate change, especially as a transition fuel source, buying much-needed time for climate-change solutions to move out of their incubation phase. Its advocates claim it is a proven, cost-competitive, and almost emission-free energy alternative.[8] Nuclear power plants operate in numerous countries around the globe and, no doubt, many will be expanding their nuclear electricity-generating capacity to meet their emissions targets.

The construction of nuclear power plants has a notorious track record and is littered with examples of cost overruns and delays. Critics have argued that the true cost of nuclear power has been underestimated as it does not involve total long-term costs of decontaminating and decommissioning power plants, as well as the ongoing management of nuclear wastes. Governments have underwritten public liabilities and the nuclear industry has relied on public subsidies—monies that could be spent more effectively elsewhere.

Another concern highlighted is that high-grade uranium supplies are finite, less than 100 years at the present rate of consumption. The availability of nuclear fuel is not necessarily the issue as potential alternatives exist to uranium if the costs become competitive and other hurdles are overcome. Fastbreeder reactors that use fissionable plutonium could eventually be brought into commercial operation. Further research may even give rise to nuclear reactors that use more abundant thorium. Realistically, greatly expanding nuclear energy is not a viable strategy in combating climate change for three main reasons:

- Adverse public opinion on safety issues and accident fears
- Enhanced threat of weapons proliferation
- Failure of the nuclear industry to put forward a convincing case for the long-term management of hazardous radioactive wastes

"The nuclear option does not make sense on any level: economically, environmentally, politically, or socially. It is too costly, too dangerous, too slow, and it has too slow an impact on global warming . . . promoting nuclear power as the solution to climate change is like advocating smoking as a cure for obesity."
—Ian Lowe, Emeritus Professor of Science, Technology and Society, Griffith University

"The true cost of nuclear energy is prohibitive, with taxpayers picking up the tab. . . and the potential for a catastrophic accident or a terrorist attack far outweighs any benefits."
—Dr. Helen Caldicott, Nuclear Power Research Institute (NPRI)

☐ Coal use is presently acceptable

☑ Coal must become cleaner

Coal is primarily used to produce electricity and heat through combustion. Of the more than five million tons consumed annually, 75 percent is used in electricity production and approximately 40 percent of all electricity production is derived from coal. Coal and petroleum use are also the main culprits and biggest contributors to carbon dioxide emissions derived from human activity. From construction to decommissioning, coal-fired power plants have a life cycle of several decades. Despite its relatively low-thermal efficiency (around 30 percent), its abundance and low-cost extraction guarantees its expanded use. With so much installed capacity and more under construction or on drawing boards, it is difficult to imagine that coal won't continue to have a significant role in the energy production mix by the middle of the twenty-first century. In China alone, one thousand megawatts of coal-derived electricity capacity is added to the national grid every few days. If coal will inevitably remain the dominant power source during the next few decades, and if carbon dioxide emission cuts of 60 percent by 2050 have been called for, then how do we tame coal?

Coal's vulnerability as an energy option will become exposed as emission schemes become widespread and the carbon price begins to increase. The only way utilities can use greater amounts of inexpensive, dirty, and easily available coal, while simultaneously making a meaningful impact on emissions, is to turn coal into gas before using it to generate electricity, and then later on capturing and storing the CO_2 emissions. Gasification increases the thermal efficiency of coal, improving its energy conversion. Integrated gasification combined-cycle (IGCC) plants are being developed, as are CCS (carbon capture and storage) techniques. These technologies will significantly increase the cost of coal-energy operations. Such plants must be designed to incorporate emission-reducing features from the onset as they cannot be retrofitted to existing coal plants. They must also be located near stable geological formations to minimize transport costs for carbon storage.

Also, remember, even under an optimistic scenario where the technical hurdles of coal gasification followed by carbon capture, separation, and storage are overcome within permissible cost structures, this is not a long-term solution as carbon is simply being buried. It does, however, buy time in the transition to less carbon-intensive energy options and allows governments to reduce their coal dependency over a more manageable time horizon.

"As a cheap and plentiful fuel, coal is likely to remain an important source of energy to a world beset by climate change."
—*The Future of Coal*, MIT Report

☐ Renewable ~~energy is unreliable~~

☑ Renewable energy offers much hope

Renewable energy sources presently provide around 13 percent of the world's energy needs. They include hydroelectricity, geothermal, biomass, wind, tidal, and solar power (both photovoltaic and thermal heating). The attractiveness of renewable energy sources is this: in the conversion of fuel to energy, they produce no net carbon dioxide emissions. They represent an ideal vehicle moving forward into a carbon-constrained world and have broad public acceptance. Putting hydropower and traditional biomass aside, as they have limitations to rapid expansion, the three renewable energies that arguably hold the most hope in meeting the climate change challenge are geothermal, wind, and solar.

Geothermal power is not widespread and relies on hydrothermal sources: naturally occurring reservoirs of hot water, steam, or rocks located near the Earth's surface. This steam can be used to spin turbines and generate electricity. An incredible amount of untapped geothermal energy is stored as heat in water and rock strata at depths of up to 10 kilometers below the Earth's surface. We are probably only several years away from seeing the commercial realization of geothermal plants harnessing energy by extracting the Earth's inner heat by what is known as "hot fractured rock geothermal technology." Experience gained in the oil industry makes these depths drillable and reachable. If the other technical hurdles are overcome, this technology may become a significant emission and waste-free renewable energy option.

Critics of renewable energy claim that some forms are unsuitable for baseload capacity[9] and that others are expensive to deploy and intermittent, for example, the wind does not blow and the sun does not shine all the time. Counterarguments are that wind and solar are decentralized energy systems that offer greater security. For wind and solar power, the main challenges are on improving conversion efficiencies and energy storage technologies, reducing operating costs, and overcoming locational objections. True, renewable energy is generally more expensive and its expansion has relied on subsidies and renewable energy targets set by governments. However, the fossil fuel industry is not paying a price for the pollution it is producing. Once carbon trading schemes take hold globally, renewable energy options will become increasingly competitive and attract investment research capital that, ultimately, will bring further cost reductions. Arguably, renewables remain the most attractive way forward in tackling energy demand in a climate-change context.

"One cubic kilometer of hot granite rock at 250 degrees has the stored energy equivalent of 40 million barrels of oil."

—Geodynamics Limited, publicly listed company exploring hot fractured rock geothermal energy

"Solar, wind are safe and clean, let's shut down the oil machine! We are here to let you know, the time has come for oil to go!"

—A chant sung at the World Petroleum Congress, Calgary, June 2000

☐ China will never comply

☑ China will come to the party

China's energy mix is disproportionately dominated by coal. Not surprisingly, it has 16 of the world's top 20 most polluted cities. Tens of thousands of Chinese die or are hospitalized as a result of pollution. The estimate is that pollution causes damage equivalent to 3 percent of China's gross domestic product. China will come to the party on climate change, simply because it has no choice. The momentum of three decades of economic reform and uninterrupted near double-digit economic growth will be jeopardized if China does not act decisively to address environmental concerns. However, environmental constraints can seriously stall China's growth trajectory, slowing the rise out of poverty for millions.

As a developing country, China has no binding emission limits under Kyoto until 2012. However,

40 percent of all CDM credits issued under the protocol have been for projects in China as it is considered a relatively low-risk investment environment. Most of these credits have come from the destruction of halogenated fluorocarbons (used as refrigerants), the most potent of greenhouse gases.

China is implementing a wide range of energy and industrial policies driven by climate-change concerns. Its eleventh five-year plan (2005–2010) calls for reducing energy intensity (energy consumption per unit of GDP), improving efficiency in the top 1,000 enterprises, retiring inefficient power and industrial plants, improving fuel economy standards, increasing energy taxes on energy-intensive products, promoting advanced technologies, and many other measures. China is striving to optimize its energy mix through diversification and greater use of natural gas, hydro, nuclear, and renewable energies, while simultaneously researching cleaner coal options. Under the National Renewable Energy Law adopted in 2005, the Chinese government has set a target of producing 16 percent of its primary energy from renewable sources by 2020. Other strategies also include limiting population growth through family planning and devoting more resources to education, training, and public awareness of climate change.

A dominant feature of China's economic success is decentralized decision-making. Broad policy guidelines might be set by the Beijing government, but administrators at the provincial and local levels are *incentivized* to achieve economic growth targets. The downside to this is overcapacities in certain industries can result due to overinvestment. To address climate change, the Chinese government must look at changing the incentives and linking them to environmental standards. Clean air and water, lower greenhouse emissions, and sustainable development need to be given greater priority.

"Climate change affects sustainable development and the well-being of all humanity. The Chinese government attaches great importance to the problem."

—Hu Jintao, President of China

"In 2008, China's vehicle standards will exceed those of the United States by a substantial margin in each vehicle class."

—Kerry Emanuel, *What We Know About Climate Change*

☐ Green is ~~green~~

☑ Green is the new black

As mentioned previously, there are firms and individuals who have a vested interest in stalling the climate-change debate. Often their methods and tactics can be detected. The overlooked, troubling side of this debate are firms and individuals with opportunistic behavior. For them, the issue is not whether climate change is happening or not. They are satisfied that the overwhelming consensus is climate change is occurring and, more important, that the public, hence, consumers, have embraced this viewpoint.

The challenge for these firms is how they can flaunt their green credentials and increase revenues through marketing and public-relations initiatives. By touting their carbon-neutral status or exaggerating the impact of their green endeavors, their aim is to attract more customers. They are aware that a sizeable market segment of environmentally conscious consumers are prepared to pay slightly more for eco-friendly products. The challenge here for the public is to discern between the genuine and the half-hearted, cosmetic, misleading, or erroneous claims. Consumers should remain skeptical and not tolerate companies that make grandiose claims about their green credentials. This is easier said than done, as most consumers are not in a position to refute these claims and, often, no requirement or process exists where these claims must be demonstrated.

This is also a problem of disclosure standards. With growing public concern for climate change, companies are expected to demonstrate improved environmental credentials and these efforts need to be communicated to a wider audience. What constitutes improved environmental initiatives can vary immensely, depending on the nature of the firm or industry. This, then, becomes an issue of interpretation if no standardized disclosure requirements exist. Unless mandatory reporting exists with consistent standards, there is scope for firms to "greenwash" their achievements.[10]

"In a vacuum of real market and policy signals, we are happy to invent our own urban myths. Fortunes are being made selling the fashion of climate change . . . in the present market

of high visibility on climate change action, companies are declaring themselves carbon neutral, although energy experts and academics are concerned the market is moving too far ahead of the regulations needed to police it."

—Matthew Warren, *The Weekend Australian*, April 21–22, 2007

☑ Climate change and investment strategy

The market for energy-generating technologies has never been an even one. Polluting fossil-fuel technologies have not had to worry about their greenhouse gas emissions and even received public subsidies. These subsidies should be reduced and redirected toward cleaner alternatives. A new landscape will take shape as the "carbon cost" becomes a driver of investment decisions. Climate change will bring about all sorts of investment opportunities and challenges, especially for financial institutions and professional service firms. New carbon markets will emerge as countries establish national emission-trading schemes. Companies affected by climate change will require advice on hedging and trading strategies to manage their costs and reduce risk. Insurance advice will also be required. It is foreseeable that directors and officers will be liable for their actions (or inactions) toward climate-change impacts.

Investment funds will most likely reassess their strategies as they rebalance their portfolios. Expect them to underweigh sectors that contain high-carbon-intensive industries with little capacity to adapt to the brave new world that will emerge. Companies poorly positioned to compete in a warming world will earn the wrath of investors. This new investment climate won't be directionless. It will be guided by fluctuations in the carbon-price signal and by breakthroughs in abatement and adaptation technologies. Market favorites will be firms focusing on delivering products and services of improved energy efficiency and those exposed to renewable and low-carbon energy sources.

In many cases, it won't be obvious which sectors will be winners or losers, as the trajectory of climate-change conditions cannot be predicted with certainty. Physical exposure risk will interrupt many industries (agriculture, tourism, insurance) if extreme weather conditions become more pronounced. Companies will be exposed to numerous other risks: regulatory, supply chain, product, and technology risks are some of them. Those that will fare better in a carbon-constrained future will not only be more astute in mitigating these risks, but they will also be more adept at commercializing technology opportunities.

"Climate change is a slow but powerful force, which will shape the economic landscape inexorably."
—John Llewellyn, Lehman Brothers

"Governments' efforts to tackle climate change are creating a 'megatrend' investment opportunity . . . investable markets are being created by governments, and these will grow significantly over the next 20 to 30 years."
—Mark Fulton, climate change strategist, Deutsche Bank

"Chief carbon officer . . . is not yet a designated term, but it is likely to become one sooner than later as carbon trading changes from being a matter of risk management, to one of management planning."
—Leon Gettler, *The Age*, November 28, 2007

☐ Change is an unwelcome constraint

☑ Formulate a strategy as change represents opportunity

With each passing day, individuals and firms will increasingly have to factor climate-change concerns into their working and nonworking lives as they execute decisions and make choices. Those who view climate-change adaptation or mitigation as an opportunity rather than a cost will become successful. Their challenge becomes one of formulating a strategy to address climate-change considerations.

A firm may view climate change as an irritating compliance cost imposed by a regulatory body and detest the additional accountability. Or, it may view this compliance cost as an opportunity to do things differently, to create a healthier work environment, to reassess processes, and to promote innovation. Depending on the industry sector, climate change may be an opportunity for a firm either to enter this sector or to leapfrog its competitors by being first to embrace a new low-carbon technology, thereby setting new performance benchmarks. First-mover advantage often is critical in establishing a position of market dominance. Another strategy for the firm should be to seek to influence the policy-development process. The competitive landscape to emerge will be determined by the new rules to be enacted by governments. Input will be sought from a variety of sources. Any firm on top of its game should have a strategy in place to make its concerns known through lobbying and public-relations efforts.

For the individual or household, climate change could be the required circuit breaker that compels them to reexamine their lifestyle. It could be the stimulus to introduce energy-saving features to one's home; the catalyst in embracing sustainable living options.[11]

Addressing climate change is sensitive and controversial because it is all about economic costs and lifestyle changes in the context of responsibilities and values. The potential for backlash and conflicting interests is enormous. If everyone is a stakeholder, how do we achieve the right level of spending? How do we find the right balance between adaptation and mitigation strategies[12] if resources are finite? To what extent are we prepared to see a reorientation of our economy? As events unfold and more information surfaces, positions and opinions also shift. The only constant appears to be change. This is precisely where opportunity comes in, trying to find a strategy—a plan of action—to deal with climate-change impacts. The rewards will go to those who are innovative, insightful, and prepared to cut a path through this complexity.

Climate change represents an opportunity to make a positive impact in many realms. This is an opportunity to make a difference to the world's most challenging problem.

"The future belongs to those who understand that doing more with less is compassionate, prosperous, and enduring, and thus more intelligent, even competitive."

—Paul Hawken, author and longtime environmental activist

→ great quote :·) to end with

~~The market can provide all the answers~~

☑ Government has a leading role to play

The accumulating scientific data indicates that significant action is required on climate change, and on an accelerated basis. Meanwhile, a widening gap is emerging between advancing scientific knowledge and the response from governments. This chasm is leading to greater levels of uncertainty for business. Businesses are developing a greater profile in this debate to influence future policy frameworks. They see it as inevitable that they must adopt policies to minimize risk and exposure to uncertainty.

Firms are anticipating tighter constraints on emissions, but they are also eagerly awaiting the emergence of new investment opportunities. They are expecting a realignment of standards, but also seeking government leadership on this life-threatening matter. Inaction means delays and higher future costs. Governments have a role to play in fostering partnerships with both the business-investor community and the public at large. Setting up a legal framework for a carbon-price signal mechanism, such as emission trading, should be of the highest priority. Encouraging innovation and investment in emerging and breakthrough technologies through grants, subsidies, and tax incentives can only hasten emission compliance efforts. Setting new industry and building standards that will enhance energy efficiency also requires government participation. Public awareness and education campaigns on climate change, and the issues associated with it, can only occur on a wide scale with government involvement.

The issue of picking technology winners is always a controversial one. Often, governments have a poor track record in this respect. Many climate-change technologies are in their infancy, all vying for increased funding, both public and private. A more prudent government approach and, in the long run, a less burdensome approach to taxpayers, is to fast-track research by providing additional funding and incentives. Assisting demonstration and pilot plants to come to fruition more quickly would also yield benefits.

To meet challenging emission trajectories, promising technology solutions must be made accessible within acceptable scale, performance, and cost parameters in faster-than-normal commercial time frames. Governments can hasten this process by devoting more resources at an early stage. This early intervention increases the probability of a technology pathway's viability surfacing sooner. Once this is apparent and the economic costs become quantifiable, private funding will follow as the investment risk involved is considerably lower.

"Without a clear policy framework that matches investment horizons, business has little incentive to invest now in newer, cleaner technologies."
—Australian Business Roundtable on Climate Change, April 2006 Report

"In the absence of policies to correct the externalities and market imperfections associated with the emission of greenhouse gases and with innovation, markets cannot be expected to deliver efficient or desirable outcomes."
—Sir Nicholas Stern

☐ ~~There is plenty of time~~

☑ Stop procrastinating, act now!

Climate change resulting from global warming is arguably the most serious threat facing humanity this century. It pits nation against nation, the developed world versus the developing world, and industry against industry. It questions individual lifestyles, consumer choices, and the world's economic order. It raises questions of intra- and intergenerational equity. The issue is so multifaceted and politically contentious that any decision made requiring immediate action will always earn the wrath of someone. How do societies seek an appropriate trade-off between the development needs of a nation-state and global responsibility? How do governments enact lifestyle-changing legislation when political short-termism is the order of the day? How should decisions be made when, on the one hand, we demand community consultation, but on the other, we do not want things in our own backyard?

With the potential consequences being so dire, what will be the solutions, both short term and long term? Some solutions are here now; they only need implementation. Others are in the process of development, while many others are yet to appear. Over time, humanity has shown a great capacity for ingenuity and adaptability in dealing with adversity. We do not want this potential to come to the foreground once some critical climax has been reached as the potential response might be quite extreme, if not too late. We run the risk of being governed by decrees issued by scientific experts because the horse has bolted and drastic measures have already become inevitable. This can be avoided if governments agree to a set of mutual responsibilities, reinforce institutions for effective cooperation, and promote the conditions for coordinated collective action in reducing climate-change risk.

Every global citizen has a responsibility to sensitize themselves to the challenge, to monitor the debate, to remain informed, to psychologically prepare themselves for changes, and to put pressure on governments to establish a more activist agenda in addressing this planetary emergency. Climate change is a moral issue where a paradigm shift is required in dealing with the problem. The business-as-usual approach has long been discredited. For the sake of future generations, new rules of engagement are required, as is swifter decision-making. As the custodians of this planet, not only does the burden lie with us, but so do the solutions through our actions.

"The science has made it quite clear. We have been feeling the impact of global warming already . . . we have resources and we have technologies. The only thing lacking is political will."
—Ban Ki-Moon, UN Secretary-General

"While climate changes run like a rabbit, world politics move like a snail: either we accelerate or we risk disaster."
—Alfonso Pecoraro Scanio, Italy's Environment Minister

"Climate change poses clear, catastrophic threats. We may not agree on the extent, but we certainly can't afford the risk of inaction."
—Rupert Murdoch, media magnate

"It's very important to understand that climate change is not just another issue in this complicated world of proliferating issues. Climate change is THE issue, which, unchecked, will swamp all the other issues."
—Ross Gelbspan, author of *Boiling Point*

"A true conservationist is a man who knows that the world is not given by his fathers, but borrowed from his children."
—John James Audubon (1785–1851), ornithologist and naturalist

"The economy is a wholly owned subsidiary of the environment, not the reverse. Without ecology, there is no economy."
—Herman Daly, American ecological economist

"Periodically, major new forces dramatically reshape the business world—as globalization and the information technology revolution have. . . . Climate change, in its complexity and potential impact, may rival them both."
—Michael E. Porter and Forest L. Reinhardt, *Harvard Business Review*, October 2007

"The only good question is: what do we do about it? The earth and its atmosphere are the cage, we are the lab rats, and if we get it wrong the first time, there will be no opportunity to repeat the study."
—Peter Doherty, Nobel Prize for Medicine (1996) recipient, on climate change

"The science of climate change has never been clearer. . . . Without further action, scientists now estimate we may be heading for temperature rises of at least three to four degrees above preindustrial levels . . . We have a window of only 10 to 15 years to avoid crossing catastrophic tipping points. . . ."

—Letter to European leaders by the British and Dutch prime ministers, Tony Blair and Jan Peter Balkenende, October 2006

Notes, Sources, and Suggested Readings

Notes

1. http://www.epa.gov/climatechange/basicinfo.html.
2. ibid.
3. A carbon sink is a reservoir that can absorb carbon dioxide from the atmosphere. Examples are forests, soils, peat, permafrost, seawater, and carbonates in deep oceans.
4. Houghton, p.28.
5. Assessment reports issued by the IPCC comprehensively outline the scientific evidence.
6. http://en.wikipedia.org/wiki/Intergovernmental_Panel_on _Climate_Change.
7. Carbon dioxide equivalent (CO_2e). Different greenhouse gases have different levels of impact on global warming. Emissions of greenhouse gases are often measured in CO_2 equivalents. A ton of each individual greenhouse gas is adjusted to be expressed in terms of how many tons of CO_2 would be needed to produce the same global impact over 100 years. *The Stern Review* quotes greenhouse gas levels based on CO_2 equivalents with respect to gases covered by the Kyoto Protocol.
8. CO_2 emissions from the mining, milling, and enrichment of low-grade uranium can approach those of a natural gas plant (Diesendorf, p.253).
9. Baseload capacity is electric power output that can be produced continuously. This is distinguished from peaking or cycling capacity.
10. See Mohr, discussion paper on "greenwashing."
11. For ideas on what can immediately be implemented at the individual or household level, suggestions are provided in references Dauncey, de Rothschild, and Reay.
12. http://www.brookings.edu/papers/2004/05globaleconomics_ mckibbin.aspx. Discussion paper on adaptation versus mitigation strategies.

Web Links

Climate Change Investment Research
http://www.jpmorgan.com/pages/jpmorgan/investbk/solutions/
research/climatechange

Hadley Centre
http://www.metoffice.gov.uk/research/hadleycentre

IPCC (Intergovernmental Panel on Climate Change)
http://www.ipcc.ch/

Pew Center on Global Climate Change
http://www.pewclimate.org/

Reports

Australian Business Climate Group, *Stepping Up: Accelerating the Deployment of Low Emission Technology in Australia*, August 2007.

Australian Business Roundtable on Climate Change, *The Business Case for Early Action*, April 2006.

The Australian Climate Group, *Climate Change: Solutions for Australia*, WWF Australia, June 2004.

Australian Greenhouse Office, Department of the Environment and Heritage, *Climate Change Impacts & Risk Management: A Guide for Business and Government*, 2006.

Richard Doornbosch and Ronald Steenblik, *Biofuels: Is the Cure Worse than the Disease?* Paris OECD, Round Table on Sustainable Development: 11–12 September 2007.

The Economist, *Cleaning Up: A Special Report on Business and Climate Change*, 2 July 2007.

Friends of the Earth Australia, *Avoiding Catastrophe: A Survey by the Carbon Equity Project*, January 2007.

The Future of Coal: An Interdisciplinary MIT Study, 2007.

The Future of Nuclear Energy: An Interdisciplinary MIT Study, 2003.

Harvard Business Review, *Forethought Special Report: Climate Business–Business Climate*, October 2007.

John Llewellyn, *The Business of Climate Change: Challenges and Opportunities*, Lehman Brothers, February 2007.

Tony Mohr, *Reputation or Reality: A Discussion Paper on Greenwashing and Corporate Sustainability*, Total Environment Centre, 2005.

UBS Wealth Management, *UBS Research Focus—Climate Change: Beyond Whether*, January 2007.

Books

Helen Caldicott, *Nuclear Power is Not the Answer to Global Warming or Anything Else* (New York: The New Press, 2006).

Paul Keith Conkin, *The State of the Earth: Environmental Challenges on the Road to 2100* (Lexington: University Press of Kentucky, 2006).

John D. Cox, *Climate Crash: Abrupt Climate Change and What It Means for Our Future* (Washington, DC: Joseph Henry Press, 2005).

Guy Dauncey and Patrick Mazza, *Stormy Weather: 100 Solutions to Global Climate Change* (Gabriola Island, BC: New Society Publishers, 2001).

Andrew E. Dessler and Edward A. Parson, *The Science and Politics of Climate Change: A Guide to the Debate* (Cambridge, UK and New York: Cambridge University Press, 2006).

Mark Diesendorf, *Greenhouse Solutions with Sustainable Energy* (Seattle: University of Washington Press, 2007).

Kerry Emanuel, *What We Know About Climate Change* (Cambridge: MIT Press, 2007).

Tim Flannery, *The Weather Makers: The History and Future Impact of Climate Change* (New York: Grove/Atlantis, 2005).

Ross Gelbspan, *Boiling Point* (New York: Basic Books, 2004).

Stan Gibilisco, *Alternative Energy Demystified* (New York: McGraw-Hill, 2007).

Dinyar Godrej, *The No-Nonsense Guide to Climate Change*. 3rd ed. (Oxford: New Internationalist Publications, 2006).

Al Gore, *An Inconvenient Truth* (New York: Rodale Books, 2006).

Clive Hamilton, *Scorcher: The Dirty Politics of Climate Change* (Melbourne: Black Inc. Agenda, 2007).

Harvard Business Review on Green Business Strategy (Boston: Harvard Business School Press, 2007).

Paul Hawken, Amory Lovins, and L. Hunter Lovins, *Natural Capitalism: Creating the Next Industrial Revolution* (Boston: Little Brown and Co., 1999).

Robert Henson, *The Rough Guide to Climate Change* (New York: Rough Guides/Penguin, 2006).

Andrew J. Hoffman and John G. Woody, *Climate Change: What's Your Business Strategy?* (Boston: Harvard Business School Press, 2008).

John Houghton, *Global Warming: The Complete Briefing*. 3rd ed. (Cambridge: Cambridge University Press, 2004).

Charles F. Kutscher (ed.), *Tackling Climate Change: Potential Carbon Emissions Reductions from Energy Efficiency and Renewable Energy by 2030* (Boulder: American Solar Energy Society, January 2007).

Ian Lowe, "Reaction Time: Climate Change and the Nuclear Option," *Quarterly Essay*, Issue 27 (Melbourne: Black Inc., 2007).

Mark Maslin, *Global Warming: A Very Short Introduction* (New York: Oxford University Press, 2004).

George Monbiot, *Heat: How to Stop the Planet Burning* (London: Allen Lane/Penguin, 2006).

Fred Pearce, *With Speed and Violence: Why Scientists Fear Tipping Points in Climate Change* (Boston: Beacon Press, 2007).

A. Barrie Pittock, *Climate Change Turning Up the Heat* (Melbourne: CSIRO Publishing, 2005).

Dave Reay, *Climate Change Begins at Home* (London: Macmillan, 2005).

Joseph J. Romm, *Hell and High Water: Global Warming, the Solution and the Politics and What We Should Do* (New York: William Morrow, 2007).

David de Rothschild, *The Live Earth Global Warming Survival Handbook: 77 Essential Skills to Stop Climate Change* (New York: Rodale Books, 2007).

Jerry Silver, *Global Warming and Climate Change Demystified* (New York: McGraw-Hill, 2008).

Nicholas Stern, *The Economics of Climate Change: The Stern Review* (New York: Cambridge University Press, 2006).

Robert Strom, *Hot House: Global Climate Change and the Human Condition* (New York: Copernicus Books, 2007).

T. H. Tietenberg, *Emissions Trading: Principles and Practice*. 2nd ed. (Washington, DC: Resources for the Future, 2006).

Ted Trainer, *Renewable Energy Cannot Sustain a Consumer Society* (Dordrecht: Springer, 2007).

108

The McGraw-Hill Mighty Managers Handbooks

The Powell Principles

by Oren Harari (0-07-144490-4)

Details two dozen mission- and people-based leadership skills that have guided Colin Powell through his nearly half-century of service to the United States.

Provides a straight-to-the-point guide that any leader in any arena can follow for unmitigated success.

How Buffett Does It

by James Pardoe (0-07-144912-4)

Expands on 24 primary ideas Warren Buffett has followed from day one.

Reveals Buffett's stubborn adherence to the time-honored fundamentals of value investing.

The Lombardi Rules

by Vince Lombardi, Jr. (0-07-144489-0)

Presents more than two dozen of the tenets and guidelines Lombardi used to drive him and those around him to unprecedented levels of success.

Packed with proven insights and techniques that are especially valuable in today's turbulent business world.

The Welch Way

by Jeffrey A. Krames (0-07-142953-0)

Draws on the career of Jack Welch to explain how workers can follow his proven model.

Shows how to reach new heights in today's wide-open, idea-driven workplace.

The Ghosn Factor

by Miguel Rivas-Micoud (0-07-148595-3)

Examines the life, works, and words of Carlos Ghosn, CEO of *Nissan* and *Renault*.

Provides 24 succinct lessons that managers can immediately apply.

How to Motivate Every Employee

by Anne Bruce (0-07-146330-5)

Provides strategies for infusing your employees with a passion for the work they do.

Packed with techniques, tips, and suggestions that are proven to motivate in all industries and environments.

The New Manager's Handbook

by Morey Stettner (0-07-146332-1)

Gives tips for teaming with your employees to achieve extraordinary goals.

Outlines field-proven techniques to succeed and win the respect of both your employees and your supervisors.

The Sales Success Handbook

by Linda Richardson (0-07-146331-3)

> Shows how to sell customers—not by what you tell them, but by how well you listen to what they have to say.

> Explains how to persuasively position the value you bring to meet the customer's business needs.

How to Plan and Execute Strategy

by Wallace Stettinius, D. Robley Wood, Jr., Jacqueline L. Doyle, and John L. Colley, Jr. (0-07-148437-X)

> Provides 24 practical steps for devising, implementing, and managing market-defining, growth-driving strategies.

> Outlines a field-proven framework that can be followed to strengthen your company's competitive edge.

How to Manage Performance

by Robert Bacal (0-07-148439-8)

> Provides goal-focused, common-sense techniques to stimulate employee productivity in any environment.

> Details how to align employee goals and set performance incentives.

Managing in Times of Change

by Michael D. Maginn (0-07-148436-1)

> Helps you to understand and explain the benefits of change, while flourishing within the new environment.

> Provides straight talk and actionable advice for teams, managers, and individuals.